Uģis Prauliņš
MISSA RIGENSIS

for unaccompanied
SATB chorus with soloists

(2001/2)

NOVELLO

© 2012 Novello & Company Limited

Order No. NOV060104

Published in Great Britain by Novello Publishing Limited

Head office: 14/15 Berners Street,
London W1T 3LJ
Tel. +44 (0)20 7612 7400
Fax +44 (0)20 7612 7545

COMPOSER'S NOTE

Missa Rigensis (*The Mass of Riga*) was composed in 2001-2 as a hymn in honour of my native city of Riga, the birthplace of so many great thoughts and romantic visions. It was written for the Riga Dom Boys' Choir (with whom I sang when I was a boy) and its conductor, Martins Klisans; the first performance took place on the 31st March 2002 in the Riga Dom Cathedral.

Ugis Praulins (b.1957, Riga, Latvia) studied at the Latvian Academy of Music. During his student years he was active as a rock musician as well as being involved in the folk music revival, later touring with his rock and folk band *Vecas Majas*. Since the 1990s he has concentrated on composing. His output includes concert and stage works and music for feature films and animation. In 1998, Praulins released his own ambient/ Latvian folk concept album *Paganu gadagramata* (*Pagan Yearbook*), which was awarded best folk album of the year in Latvia. In 1999, the Riga Dom Boys' Choir directed by Martins Klisans recorded the concept album *Odi et amo*, likewise awarded best album of the year. Recent works for voices include: *Imagination* (*The Land of My Heart*) for the 2011 International Festival of Children's Choirs; *The Nightingale* for Danish recorder virtuoso Michala Petri and Danish National Vocal Ensemble conducted by Stephen Layton (2010); *To the Light* (*Asato Maa Sat Gamaya*) for the Uetersen Male Chorus and saxophone; and *Venus et Amor* for the Gaudeamus Male Chorus and instrumental ensemble.

The first recording of *Missa Rigensis* was made by the Riga Dom Boys' Choir and released in 2002 on the CD *Gariga muzika Doma baznica* (Sacred Music at the Dom Cathedral), PMP3155. In 2010, Trinity College Choir, Cambridge under Stephen Layton recorded *Missa Rigensis* as part of the Baltic Exchange collection, Hyperion CDA67747

MISSA RIGENSIS

I KYRIE ELEISON

UĢIS PRAULIŅŠ

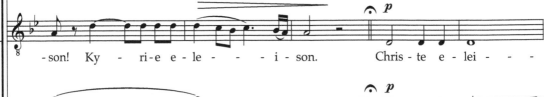

Tempo I, rubato (♩ = 72–76)

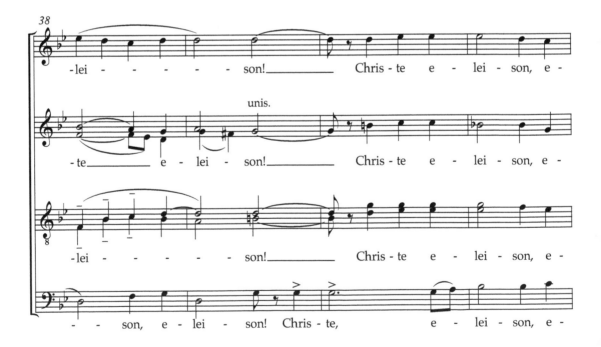

Tempo II

TENOR SOLO

allargando
42
ff
fff
- le - i - son, Chris - te e - lei - - - - - - - - son!
- lei - son, Chris - te e - lei - - - - - - - - son!
- lei - son, Chris - te e - lei - son, e - lei - - - son!
- lei - son, Chris - te e - lei - son, e - lei - - - son!
Tempo II
TENOR SOLO
47
ppp meditativo
Mm, mm
51
TENOR SOLO
Ky - ri - e e - le - i - son, e - le - i - son.

II GLORIA
GLORIA IN EXCELSIS

Leggiero, distinto ($\quad$ = 70)

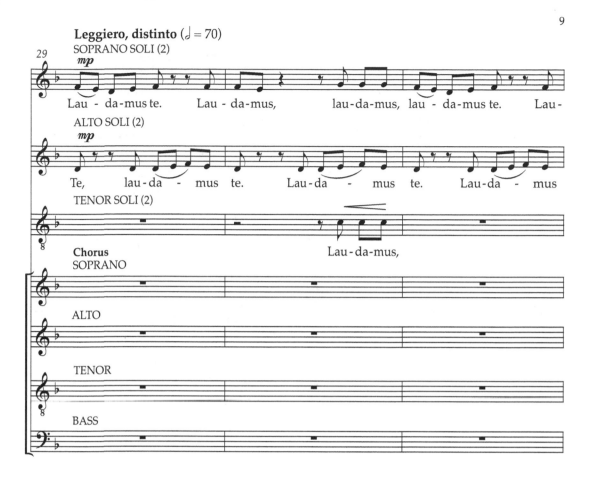

Sostenuto ♩ = 100

allargando a tempo, ma rubato

DOMINE DEUS

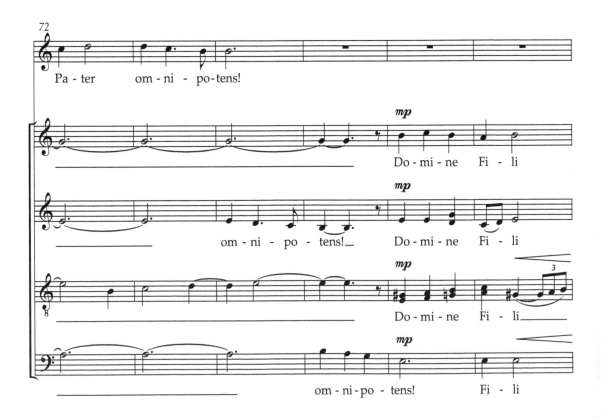

Chorus

SOPRANO
Qui tol - lis pec - ca - ta mun - di,

ALTO
Qui tol - lis pec - ca - ta mun - di,

TENOR
Qui tol - lis pec - ca - ta mun - di! Mi-se-re-re no - bis.

BASS
Qui tol - lis pec - ca - ta mun - di! Mi-se-re-re no - bis.

SOPRANO SOLI (2)
Sus-ci-pe de-pre-ca-ti - o-nem nos-trum, sus-ci-pe de-pre-ca-ti - o-nem

ALTO SOLI (2)
Sus-ci-pe de-pre-ca-ti - o-nem nos-trum, sus-ci-pe de-pre-ca-ti - o-nem

TENOR SOLI (2)
Sus-ci-pe de-pre-ca-ti - o-nem nos-trum, sus-ci-pe de-pre-ca-ti - o-nem

BASS SOLI (2)
Sus-ci-pe de-pre-ca-ti - o-nem nos-trum, sus-ci-pe de-pre-ca-ti - o-nem

attacca

QUONIAM

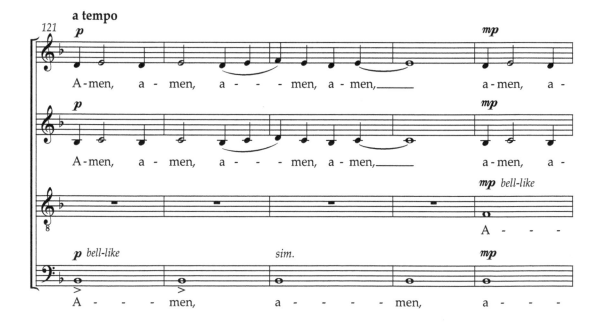

III CREDO
CREDO IN UNUM DEUM

Solenne ♩ = 60

DEUM DE DEO

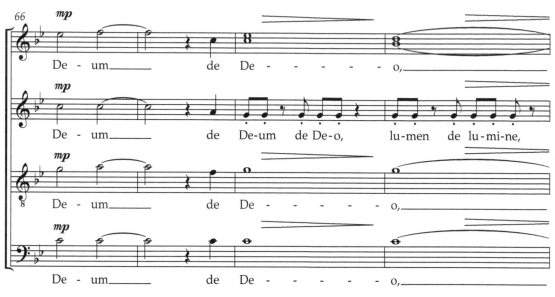

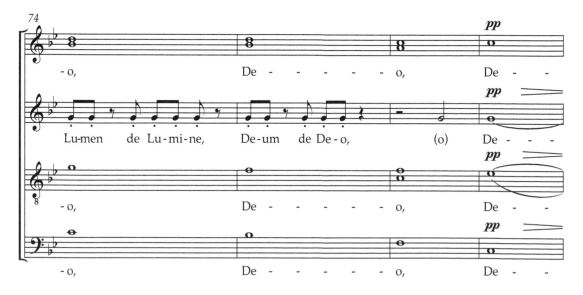

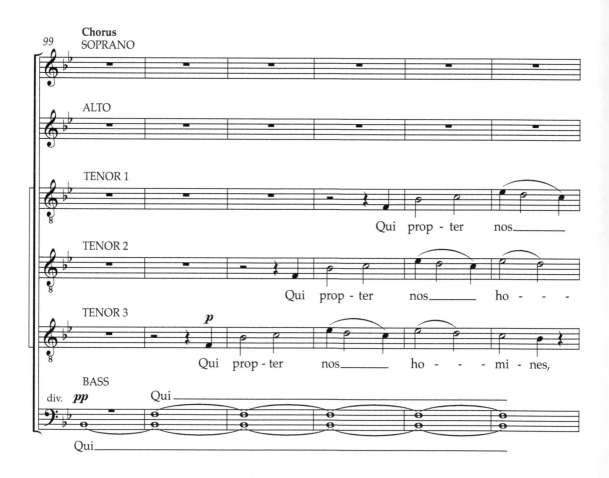

CRUCIFIXUS

* Basses sing the word 'Pon-ti-o' freely on the witten notes, with a nasal tone

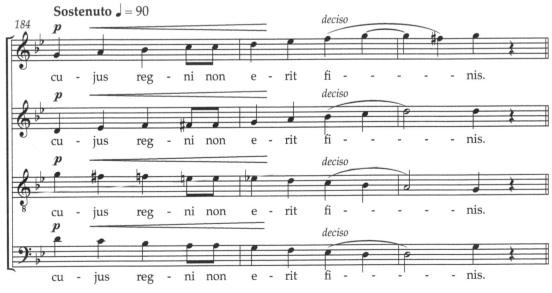

attacca

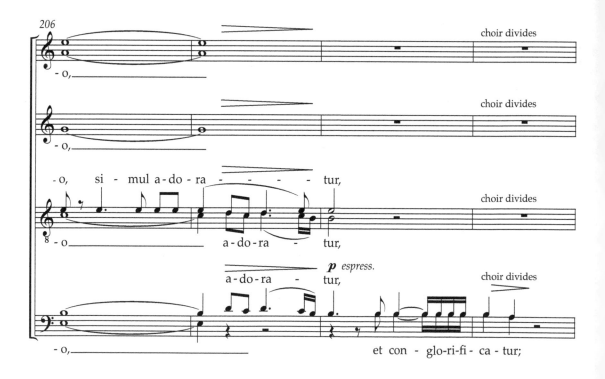

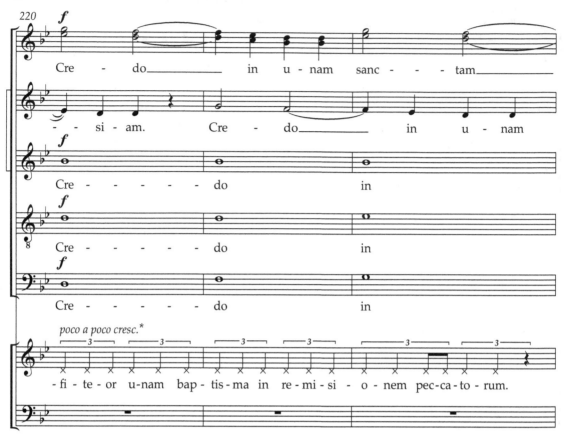

* Choir 2 gradual *crescendo* to **ff** at bar 243

44

238
sanc - - tam ca - tho - li - cam et a - - - - -
in u - nam sanc - tam ca - tho - li -
in u - - - - nam
in u - - - - nam ca - tho - - - - -
in u - - - - nam ca - tho - - - - -
- o - nem pec-ca-to - rum. Et ex - pec - to re-sur-rec-ti - o-nem mor-tu-
- o - nem pec-ca-to - rum. Et ex - pec - to re-sur-rec-ti-o - nem mor-tu-
241
- - pos - to - li - cam Ec - cle - - - si - am.
-cam et a - - - pos - to - li - cam.
sanc - tam, sanc - - - - - tam.
- li - cam sanc - - - - - tam.
- li - cam sanc - - - - - tam.
ff
mp quasi sospirando
- o-rum, et vi-tam ven-tu - ri sae-cu - li. A-men.
ff
mp quasi sospirando
- o - rum, et vi-tam ven-tu - ri sae-cu - li. A - men.

46

IV SANCTUS

Con grandezza ♩ = 84

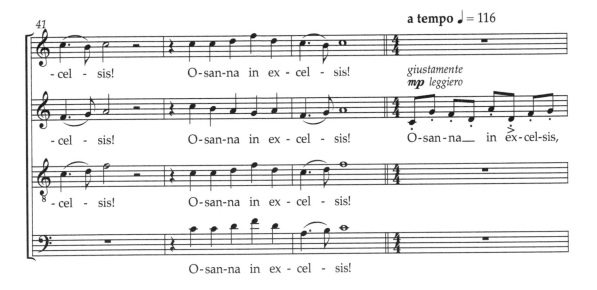

50

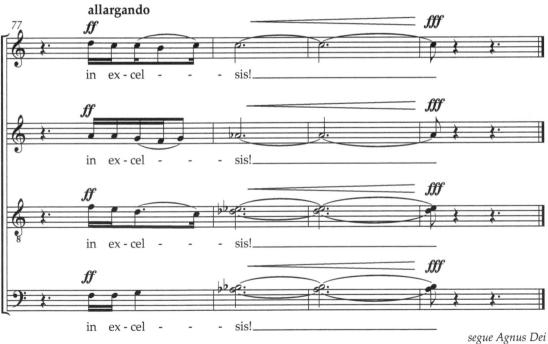

segue Agnus Dei

V AGNUS DEI

PRAYER *ad lib.*